Yorkshire Dales
PANORAMAS

STUNNING PHOTOGRAPHS OF THE NATIONAL PARK

JOHN POTTER

MYRIAD BOOKS LONDON

CONTENTS

DALES NORTH

Wensleydale and Swaledale lie at the heart of the northern Dales and are famous for their spring meadows and field barns such as those at Gunnerside and Muker. The more remote, 'tributary' dales of Arkengarthdale and Coverdale are full of hidden treasures with wide open moors dotted with tiny hamlets

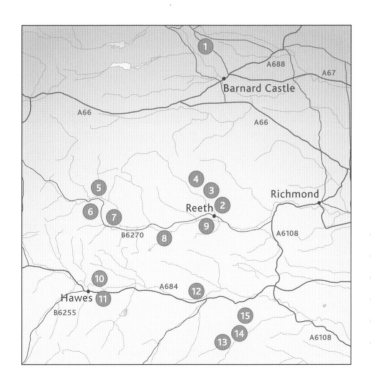

OPPOSITE – MUKER MEADOWS, SWALEDALE
Traditional late 18th-century and early 19th-century stone field barns and drystone walls abound in the countryside around Muker

BOWLEES

The tiny hamlet of Bowlees lies between Middleton-in-Teesdale and the magnificent High Force waterfall, just off the busy B6277 that links Alston to Barnard Castle. This is an area with a rich geology and spectacular scenery. It is important for rare birds such as the black grouse and many species of rare flowering plants such as globe flower and spring gentian. There is a visitor centre here providing souvenirs, light refreshments and a picnic site.

ARKENGARTHDALE

Arkengarthdale, pictured here from close to the minor moors road that weaves its way north through the dale, was once the centre of a thriving local lead-mining industry. A tributary valley of Swaledale running north from Reeth, it is a remote, peaceful and unspoilt valley. In the distance to the right Low Moor is peppered with the remains of old lead mines, and on the lower slopes nestles the oddly named hamlet of Booze.

ARKLE TOWN

Arkle Town, a tiny hamlet in the parish of Arkengarthdale, is a third of a mile south-east of Langthwaite on the road to Reeth, seen here from Scotty Hill on the minor road that links Langthwaite to Booze. There is an old graveyard at Arkle Town and many of the headstones are to be found leaning up against the drystone wall beside the main road. The drystone wall in the photograph, though in need of repair, provides an attractive foreground to the view.

LANGTHWAITE

The picturesque village of Langthwaite is seen here from the steep minor road that winds up around Scotty Hill through the quaintly named hamlet of Booze, and on to Booze Moor. Curiously, Booze does not have an inn but Langthwaite does – the cosy and welcoming Red Lion which was used extensively in the filming of the television series *All Creatures Great and Small*. At the church of St Mary's in Langthwaite it is traditional to lock the gates during weddings and for local children to gather outside – the gates are only unlocked and the wedding party freed when money is tossed to the waiting children!

SWALEDALE

These attractive Dales' barns are situated between Aygill and Thorns Green, just east of the B6270, a minor road that links Thwaite to Keld in Upper Swaledale. There is a disused quarry in the valley bottom here, and beyond the lower slopes of Kisdon Hill rise steeply to a summit of 1637ft (499m). A very popular circular walk around Kisdon Hill takes in the villages of Keld, Muker and Thwaite and includes a short stretch of the Pennine Way.

KELD

The small village of Keld nestles snugly in the hills at the head of Swaledale. Its pretty stone cottages are clustered around a tiny square, and the hamlet is the crossover point of the Coast-to-Coast and Pennine Way footpaths. Keld is an ancient settlement – its name derives from the old Norse word 'keld', meaning spring. There are many waterfalls along the river Swale near Keld, the closest being Catrake Force and Kisdon Force. This view of the village as the sun sets to the west is from Shotlathe along the Pennine Way.

KISDON HILL

The limestone mass of Kisdon Hill stands proud at the western head of Swaledale. There are many fabulous walks on and around this magnificent hill including the long-distance footpath the Pennine Way. The nearby villages of Keld, Muker and Thwaite offer weary ramblers a welcome break with tearooms, inns and lanes full of characterful cottages to explore at a more leisurely pace. This viewpoint is from Kisdon Hill looking south towards Muker.

GUNNERSIDE

Gunnerside is a traditional Swaledale village in a stunning location. The dale is quite narrow and in the valley bottom there is an attractive patchwork of fields, drystone walls and barns. In early summer these wildflower meadows are a vibrant sea of colour, and a delight to walk through. Gunnerside Gill joins the river Swale here and leads to the remains of Sir Francis Mine and Melbrecks Moor. The windswept fells around Gunnerside are remote and beautiful, offering walkers spectacular views. In the far distance at the head of Swaledale Great Shunner Fell reaches the lofty height of 2350ft (716m).

HARKERSIDE PLACE

The small Dales town of Reeth is situated above the river Swale at the point where Arkengarthdale and Swaledale meet and is surrounded by lovely riverside and country walks. Fringed with fine 18th-century stone houses the large village green is the focal point both for the local farming community and the many visitors who come to soak up the atmosphere and view the magnificent scenery.

HARDRAW COUNTRYSIDE

Wensleydale is famous the world over for its cheese. This lovely view of snow-covered fields and drystone walls, near Hardraw, was taken from a vantage point looking south towards Hawes where the Wensleydale Creamery is located. The village of Hardraw has a hidden treasure behind the Green Dragon Inn. At 96ft (29m) Hardraw Force waterfall is the highest single drop waterfall in England. Reached along a deep-sided gorge a couple of hundred metres from the inn, the acoustics are so good in the gorge that a brass band contest is held there every year.

WENSLEYDALE BARN

This attractive barn is located beside the A684 Leyburn to Sedbergh road, near Burtersett Bottoms a little over half a mile from Hawes. Traditional late 18th and early 19th-century barns and drystone walls are a much-loved feature of the landscape in Wensleydale. The field barns (or 'laithes') house cattle and the hay to feed them during the harsh winter months, and the walls enclose grazing land. Winters in Wensleydale can be very harsh and Swaledale sheep are a hardy breed with coarse wool and the ability to seek out grass on which to graze practically anywhere.

AYSGARTH FALLS

Aysgarth village is situated seven miles (12km) west of Leyburn on the A684 and is famous for its spectacular waterfalls. They cascade down a series of huge limestone steps and after heavy spring showers, as seen here, create a thunderous and breathtaking spectacle for the visitor. There are some delightful walks through the woods along the river Ure at Aysgarth, and in early spring a beautiful white carpet of wood anemones appears.

BRAIDLEY

Coverdale is a blissfully quiet and unspoilt dale. It consists of a series of tiny picturesque hamlets and farmsteads along the long and winding minor road that links Middleham in Lower Wensleydale to Kettlewell in Wharfedale. All along the valley the river Cover is fed by a multitude of small gills and springs. Braidley is a tiny hamlet just over a mile west of the larger village of Horsehouse. The distant peak of Little Whernside at 1982ft (604m) is a prelude to Great Whernside just over the horizon, and both are linked by footpaths from Braidley and nearby Arkleside.

SWINESIDE

This view of Swineside and, beyond, West Scrafton Moor is from the roadside just a third of a mile west of the village of Carlton, where the road branches off to West Scrafton. The villages of Carlton, Melmerby, Caldbergh, Gammersgill and West Scrafton are linked by several delightful low-level footpaths, and there are a number of much longer and more demanding paths leading up over the moor tops north to Wensleydale and south to Nidderdale. The moor tops in this area have many disused mines and old workings as well as grouse butts and ancient field systems and settlements.

Coverdale Tarn, just below the summit of Great Haw at 1778ft (542m), though relatively small, offers walkers exhilarating views of Coverdale.

CARLTON

Coverdale is a tributary valley situated midway between Upper Nidderdale and Lower Wensleydale. The river Cover winds its way sedately down the dale to join the river Ure at Ulshaw just south of Middleham. At the head of the valley the minor road to Kettlewell in Wharfedale passes between Great Whernside (2310ft/704m) and Buckden Pike (2303ft/702m). Carlton is surrounded by superb walking country and is just a short drive from the nearby Dales towns of Richmond, Leyburn, Hawes and Middleham.

DALES SOUTH

Malhamdale, Wharfedale and Littondale contain some of Britain's most dramatic limestone scenery including the Three Peaks, Malham Cove and Ingleton Waterfalls

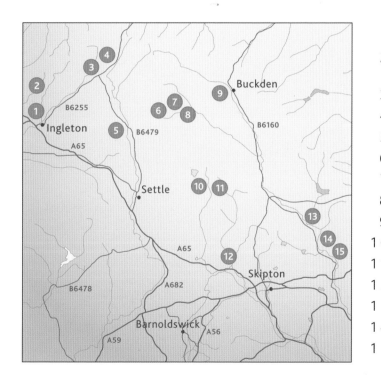

OPPOSITE – MALHAM COVE

The limestone scenery of the Yorkshire Dales is seen at its most spectacular at Malham Cove with its dramatic cliffs and pavements

INGLETON WATERFALLS

Ingleton is blessed with some of the most spectacular waterfall and woodland scenery in the country. A breathtaking five-mile walk leads through ancient oak woodland and glorious Dales scenery, and is only a stone's throw away from Ingleton. Two rivers come together here: the river Twiss flows down Kingsdale and the river Doe flows down from Chapel Le Dale. Both rivers cascade over and through a series of amazing waterfalls and plunge pools. The geology and flora in this area is diverse and rare. The largest and most famous waterfall, Thornton Force, just a short walk from the car park in Ingleton, has a drop of 46ft (14m).

KINGSDALE AND THE CHEESE PRESS STONES

Situated in the very heart of limestone country are the dramatic Cheese Press stones in Kingsdale. Set against a distant view of Ingleborough, one of the world famous Three Peaks at 2372ft (723m), these erratic boulders cry out to be photographed or painted. Whernside, at 2415ft (736m), the highest of the Three Peaks, though not as dramatic in profile, can be seen rising gradually on the left, towards the northern head of Kingsdale, where the minor road runs over into Deepdale, and then onto Dentdale. The western side of Kingsdale has many fine potholes including Bull Pot, Jingling Pot, Rowten Pot and Yordas Cave.

RIBBLEHEAD VIADUCT

The 72-mile (115 km) Settle-Carlisle railway line is one of the most picturesque in Britain and runs through Ribblesdale offering dramatic views of Whernside and Pen-y-Ghent. First constructed in the early 1870s, the line was renovated and re-opened on 19th December 2000. This route was the last great mainline railway to be built in England and it consists of 72 miles of track with 17 major viaducts spanning the ravines and 14 tunnels. The magnificent Ribblehead viaduct just to the north-west of Ribblehead station is viewed here from Runscar Hill close to the B6255 Ingleton to Hawes road. The viaduct is 104ft high (32m), 1200ft long (365m) and has 24 arches.

INGLEBOROUGH

Ingleborough, the second highest of the Three Peaks, is pictured here shrouded in low cloud on a bitterly cold winter's day, in a photograph taken from Runscar Scar just below Runscar Hill. Ingleborough has a very distinctive shape due to the local geology. Its profile is formed by a broad cap of millstone grit on top of a broader plateau of carboniferous limestone. The lower slopes have many complex and cavernous caves and potholes where streams running off the upper slopes disappear underground. Gaping Gill pot on the western flank of Ingleborough offers the expert potholer a real challenge.

RIBBLESDALE

Although it can be difficult to reach remote locations in the Dales in winter, the rewards are usually well worth the effort. This lone tree near Horton in Ribblesdale on a very cold and overcast winter's day provided the perfect focal point for a simple yet very evocative image. Almost monochrome in colour it illustrates superbly how beautiful winter scenes like this can be.

PEN-Y-GHENT

This enticing view of Pen-y-Ghent from Dale Head, on the remote Stainforth to Littondale minor road, is actually taken from the Pennine Way. The long-distance footpath follows this dead-end track for a short distance then goes up and over the summit at 2277ft (694m), and down to the village of Horton in Ribblesdale from where the famous Three Peaks race starts. The Ribble Way joins the Pennine Way for a few miles in Ribblesdale and then the Pennine Way goes north to Hawes in Wensleydale. Horton is well known for its association with Yorkshire's 'Big Three', and the café provides a useful stop for walkers.

FOXUP

Littondale is a delightful dale branching off north-west of Wharfedale, barely two miles south of Kettlewell. There are four settlements in the Dale: Arncliffe, Litton, Halton Gill and Foxup, which is the most remote. Cosh Beck and Foxup Beck feed the infant river Skirfare here and the hamlet is made up of a scattering of stone cottages and farms. All around Foxup the high fells shelter this small settlement. This viewpoint is from Low Bergh looking north over the hamlet towards Ber Gill and Eller Carr Moss.

HALTON GILL

The village of Halton Gill has a beautiful location at the head of Littondale. Surrounded and sheltered by Horse Head Moor, Plover Hill and Cow Close Fell the settlement stands proud, just above the valley floor near to the infant river Skirfare. The enterprising villagers in this tiny hamlet benefit from a very healthy drinking water supply which is drawn from a moorland spring, thanks to a grant from the rural enterprise scheme. The village can be seen here over the gate from the footpath to Foxup.

BUCKDEN MEADOWS

In the past the small village of Buckden, which is situated at the foot of Buckden Pike (2300ft/702m) in upper Wharfedale, was famous for hunting; it was ideally placed, being close to the wild and open expanses of Langstrothdale Chase. It was also used as a staging post for travellers going north to Wensleydale, Bishopdale and Langstrothdale. The wildflower meadows in the valley by the river Wharfe are a vibrant and colourful spectacle in spring and wonderful to walk through along the Dales Way, the long-distance footpath. Near the summit of Buckden Pike a memorial stone marks the place where, in 1942, members of a Polish aircrew lost their lives.

MALHAM PAVEMENT

Around 15,000 years ago Malhamdale was covered with glaciers and ice sheets. The ice scoured away all the soil to expose the limestone pavements to the elements. This classic limestone pavement above Malham Cove has hundreds of huge limestone blocks or 'clints', and deep fissures or 'grykes' which were formed over thousands of years by cracks in the rock being gradually opened up as the limestone (calcium carbonate) dissolved through weathering. The steep compact walls of the cove provide climbers with some of the best climbing in the Pennines – Yosemite, Cadenza and Obsession are the names the climbers have given to some of their favourite routes.

MALHAMDALE

Malhamdale is one of the most popular tourist spots in the Yorkshire Dales. Today, hill farming and tourism go hand in hand as the main activities in the area. Malham village, in the middle distance, was referred to in the Domesday Book as 'malgun' and it has been a settlement for at least a thousand years. Sheriff Hill, the location of this image, is surrounded by ancient field systems and settlements, but they are often difficult to see at ground level.

GARGRAVE

The Pennine Way long-distance footpath, the infant river Aire and the Leeds-Liverpool Canal pass through, or by, Gargrave, a small market town just west of Skipton on the busy A65 Skipton to Kirkby Lonsdale road. The nearby bustling market town of Skipton has a Norman castle and a wide variety of shops, galleries and tearooms, while the delightful village of Embsay just six miles (9km) away has its very own steam railway. Built in 1888 the Embsay and Bolton Abbey steam railway is lovingly cared for by volunteers from the Yorkshire Dales Railway Museum Trust, and special events take place all year round.

WHARFEDALE

Many of the scenes in the film *Calendar Girls* were filmed in Wharfedale. Burnsall was used as the location for the annual village show, although in the film it was referred to as the 'Kilnsey Show', Kilnsey being further up the dale. This view across Wharfedale from Rowan Tree Crag, looking towards Hartlington Hall and Kail Hill, was taken after a light sprinkling of snow. Low warm winter light reveals the unmistakeable character of this unique and beautiful landscape.

STRID WOOD

Strid Wood, situated midway between Bolton Priory and Barden Tower in Wharfedale, is unique. It has been designated as a Site of Special Scientific Interest because it is the largest remnant of acidic woodland in the county, having rare flora, particularly lichens. The woodland was opened to the public in 1810 by the local rector, William Carr, who gained permission from the Duke of Devonshire. Paths were created through the woods at this time. This is one such path, which leads down to the famous 'Strid', a narrow gorge through which the river Wharfe gushes and roars with great ferocity.

VALLEY OF DESOLATION

The Valley of Desolation is a tributary valley to Wharfedale, branching off from Strid Wood. Posforth Gill runs through the valley and is fed by a number of smaller gills and springs on Barden Fell. There are some very picturesque waterfalls along this pleasant woodland ravine and a delightful walk up through the valley leads on to the rocky outcrop of Simon's Seat, a prominent and well-known landmark in the area which towers over the quiet and unspoilt village of Appletreewick.

DALES EAST

The greener, gentler valleys of Uredale, Wensleydale and Nidderdale provide sumptuous scenery particularly around Jervaulx Abbey, Pateley Bridge and Ripon, with its picturesque canal

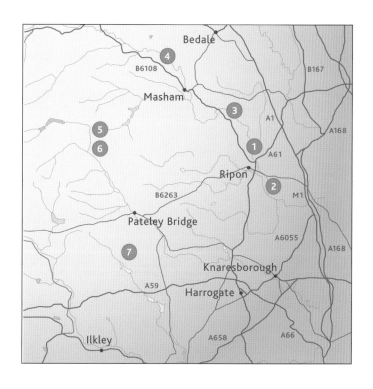

OPPOSITE – HARVESTING AT WEST TANFIELD

A combine harvester hard at work in the fields near West Tanfield at the eastern end of Wensleydale

RIPON RIVERSIDE

The attractive town of Ripon, 11 miles (18km) north of Harrogate is a gateway to the eastern Dales. Behind these riverside houses on the banks of the Ure is Ripon Cathedral. St Wilfred first built a church here over 1,300 years ago but the present building is the fourth to have been established on this site. The church did not achieve cathedral-status until 1836 when the diocese of Ripon was created. Ripon has three museums – the Courthouse Museum, the Prison and Police Museum and the Workhouse Museum of Poor Law. The Courthouse Museum featured in Yorkshire Television's popular series *Heartbeat*.

RIPON CANAL

The canal at Ripon was constructed to connect Ripon to the river Ure at Oxclose Lock and then via the river Ouse to the Humber and the other waterways of Yorkshire. The cut runs for approximately two and a half miles (4km) and has three locks. There is a large marina on the south side of the city close to the racecourse with visitors' moorings. Fourteen days of flat racing are staged between April and August at Yorkshire's Garden Racecourse each year – in fact, racing has been part of Ripon's life since 1664.

WEST TANFIELD

The countryside in lower Wensleydale and Uredale is much more pastoral than in the northern Dales with picturesque villages surrounded by gentle rolling fields and woodland. West Tanfield has a magnificent setting seen here from the stone bridge that crosses the gently flowing river Ure. The Marmion Tower and St Nicholas' church are clearly visible on the far bank.

76   JERVAULX ABBEY

Jervaulx Abbey is a privately-owned Cistercian abbey, situated just east of the A6108 between Masham and Leyburn. Founded in 1156, the abbey was ruined after the Dissolution in 1537. Despite its condition, enough remains of the ivy-covered crumbling walls to remind us of the simple yet austere lives of the 'white monks'. A delightful feature of this site today is the large number of wildflowers decorating the ancient stones and the surrounding parkland. The ruins are believed to be host to around 200 different species.

GOUTHWAITE RESERVOIR

This photograph looks down from Thrope Plantation towards Gouthwaite Reservoir which is constructed on the river Nidd, a short distance above Pateley Bridge. The plantation is located one and a half miles (2km) from Lofthouse close to the minor road that links Lofthouse to Masham in Lower Wensleydale. The area around the reservoir is a bird-lover's paradise with many birds of prey and a variety of waders. The moors in Nidderdale are host to nationally important populations of golden plover, lapwing and red grouse.

LOFTHOUSE

Lofthouse is a small and pretty Dales village situated near Middlesmoor and How Stean Gorge in Upper Nidderdale. Nidderdale has been designated as an Area of Outstanding Beauty and one can easily see why when looking out across the dale towards Stean Moor and Ramsgill Moor from Cockle Hill above the village. How Stean Gorge is a steep-sided ravine up to 80 feet (24m) deep in places with a summer canopy of hazel, oak and ash trees. There are huge boulders to scramble over and nearby caves to explore.

PATELEY BRIDGE

This distant view of Pateley Bridge from near Ravens Nest, above Fishpond Wood, shows just what a glorious setting this popular Dales town enjoys. Originally a mining village, the market town of Pateley Bridge has developed into a thriving regional tourist attraction and focal point for the local farming community. Its narrow main street is adorned with elegant dark gritstone buildings and there are many quaint cobbled courtyards packed with gift shops, galleries and tearooms.

DALES WEST

The western Dales straddle the border of Cumbria and the southern Lake District. The region has its own distinct personality and ranges from green valleys to wild windswept moorland

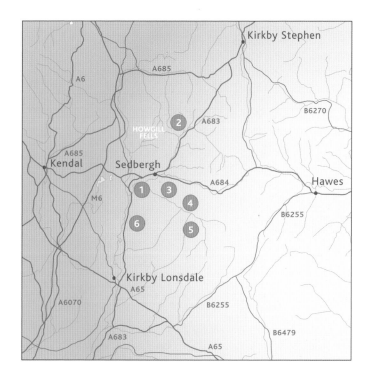

OPPOSITE – THE HOWGILL FELLS
The rounded hills of the Howgill Fells form a dramatic barrier between the north-west edge of the Dales and the uplands of Cumbria

HOME FELL

The Howgills are a dominant and unforgettable feature in the landscape marking the point where the more gentle fells of the north-west Dales meet the higher mountains of south-east Cumbria. The Howgills are seen here rising up behind the small town of Sedbergh from Holme Fell close to Catholes Farm and Bunkhouse Barn. The Howgill Fells are in Cumbria and are the only part of the Dales national park outside the Yorkshire county boundary.

HOWGILL FELLS

Taken from the roadside near the Cross Keys Inn on the Sedbergh to Kirkby Stephen road, this is one of the best views of the Howgills. In the centre of the hills lies Cautley Spout, Britain's highest waterfall, where Red Gill Beck tumbles over the edge of Cautley Crags from the shoulder of the Calf – the highest of the Howgill Fells at 2217 feet (676m). The buildings shown are at Low Haygarth Farm which is used as a trekking and trail-riding centre.

DENTDALE

The Dales Way long-distance footpath linking Ilkley in West Yorkshire to Windermere in the Lake District is essentially a valley walk. The 85-mile (137km) long path takes in some of the finest scenery in England with the Dent to Sedbergh section being particularly enjoyable. The path follows the river Dee along the western side of the valley bottom crossing over at Rash Bridge, a short distance down the valley from this viewpoint, before taking a detour through Sedbergh and then on to the Lake District.

RASH FARM

Rash Farm is situated two miles (3km) from Sedbergh on the road to Dent. The farm stands below the summit of Holme Knott (1150ft/350m) and is photographed from Moser Hill on a footpath linking the road to the Dales Way higher up the fell. The path continues to wind its way around the lower slopes of Long Rigg before going through the tiny hamlet of Millthrop and then on to Sedbergh.

DENTDALE COTTAGES

Farms and cottages in Dentdale are almost always painted white, in the Cumbrian style, in contrast to the warm natural stone buildings usually found in the lower Yorkshire Dales. The village of Dent has everything one would expect the perfect Dales village to have – cobbled streets, pretty cottages, tearooms and pubs serving real ale. Dent even has its own brewery. This photograph looks north-west from just below Combe Scar on a clear day. In the distance the Howgill Fells can be seen clearly on the horizon and in the middle distance are Helms Knott and Long Rigg ridge which leads down to Millthrop and Sedbergh.

BRIGFLATTS

This Quaker Friends Meeting House at Brigflatts, half a mile from Sedbergh on the A683 Kirkby Lonsdale road, was built by the villagers in 1675. At this time, the village was a thriving and mostly self-sufficient community of around 75 people who ran their own cottage industry relying principally on flax weaving. In 1881 a raised wooden floor was fitted to allow water from the village pond to flow through the meeting house without wetting the feet of the congregation! The poet Basil Bunting (1900-1985) is buried in the Quaker graveyard in the village.

First published in 2006 by Myriad Books Limited 35 Bishopsthorpe Road, London SE26 4PA

Photographs and text copyright © John Potter

John Potter has asserted his right under the Copyright, Designs and Patents Act 1998 to be identified as the author of this work.

ISBN 1 904 736 23 8   Designed by Phillip Appleton   Printed in China   www.myriadbooks.com